Gianni, Jan & Marcello Liscia

The Book of Happiness

A work and reflection diary

Illustrations:
Herman Reichold

1st edition, 2018

Imprint

© 2018 Gianni, Jan & Marcello Liscia

Text: Layout & Bookcover:

Biographiewerkstatt Böddeker   Franziska Eikel

Ellerstrasse 26, 33100 Paderborn   Liscia Consulting GbR

Telefon: 05293 - 9327816   Friedrich-List-Str. 42, 33100 Paderborn

Print and publishers: Books on Demand, Norderstedt

ISBN: 978-3-7528-5829-7

Just be happy

Happiness is also attitude-business. It is a matter of accepting the status quo – an essential building block to happiness, in our opinion. This has nothing to do with resigning to your fate. No, it is about truly accepting things you cannot change, no matter what you do. It makes no sense to cry over spilled milk, brooding only feeds the fire of negativity, while making it impossible to let go of the past and move ahead. A terrible waste of time.

The British say, "Love it, change it or leave it." But not every co-worker has the luxury to change things, particularly during transitional processes. Depending on her position in the hierarchy, she can influence decisions or not. When she can't, her only choice is to bite the bullet, either love it or leave it. She must decide how she will deal with the situation for her future. Mourning the past will get her nowhere.

When she does look back, she should keep her eyes on the positive aspects, the reverse gap, i.e. the period during which she was successful or overcame difficulties.

Many people focus their attention on the future. This is basically a good thing, but also entails putting off happiness, treating it as a reward – reaped sometime in the future – for deeds well done. We frequently hear such statements like, "When I retire I will have more time for my family." Or, "Let me finish this project first, then I'll relax."

The problem is, this approach keeps us from actually attaining our just rewards. The moment they are in reach, we take on another task, pushing the longed-for respite or pleasurable event further into the future. This is called a future gap, the time between the present moment and the future reward. And it explains why we are perpetually dissatisfied. Happy today? No, but maybe tomorrow, when I have done this, that and the other thing. I might have moments of satisfaction, but happy I am not.

We prefer to look at the reverse gap before setting new goals for the future. We review the last 2, 3 or 4 years, asking, what is better now? What has changed for the better during this time? What makes you happy now? What made you happy then? Focusing on the positive past, you experience happiness. You are proud of and satisfied with yourself.

When planning your future gap, you will automatically include the things that turned up in your reverse gap – that which made you happy in the past and wish to take with you into the future. Naturally, you want to achieve your goals, but they may not be so high flying as they once were. And that's the whole point, your happiness is also part of the plan, integrated into the space between goal and reward, closing the gap.

This model works particularly well with people who have recognizably evolved in a positive direction. All the same, even disastrous strokes of fate may, in retrospect, have their positive attributes. You may have a few scars to tell the tale, but you also now know who your faithful friends are and on whom you can rely. Negative experiences can certainly turn out to be valuable, when they serve to make you stronger. Perhaps, later on, you might just realign your priorities; placing less weight on accrued wealth, a luxurious lifestyle and higher status, and focusing more on the life-lessons learned.

Ever since the extreme athlete Joey Kelly spoke at our *Think Tank* in October 2016 – and again at our February 2018 *Think Tank* – giving profoundly fascinating lectures on his experience with endurance sports and his time with the Kelly Family, we have been following his career and that of his family with interest.

During the 1990s, the Kelly Family played in front of capacity audiences in mega-venues, selling several million recordings. Upon their father's death in 2002, the family fell apart, the millions were lost, and the brothers and sisters split up, each going their separate ways for the most part. Later on, independently of one another, each retold the perils of their popularity; the intense pressure, the loss of privacy, the limited freedom, and the overall burden, as most of them were still very young at the time. Still, music remained an important aspect in their lives, some successfully launching solo careers. This time around, though, they wanted to leave the nineties behind and go back to the roots. The Kelly Family began as buskers.

In his book *Streetkid: Fluch und Segen, ein Kelly zu sein / The Curse and Blessing of Being a Kelly*, Jimmy Kelly explained his motivation.

"I certainly didn't want to go back into show business. I'd seen enough to know that all that glitters, is not gold. [...] I wanted to get away from all that superficial glamour and tinsel. [...] I had long felt the desire to return to the street, where I had been happy. [...] Usually, you only come back to fundamental desires when the surrounding circumstances change drastically. Who would leave their comfort zone voluntarily? [...] Every time an athlete suffers defeat, he immediately returns to basic training, again and again. Monks constantly return to the source of devotion. The Kelly Family was originally a grass root band, playing for the people. So, I thought, if I could earn enough on the street to support my family, I would have won back a bit of happiness."[1]

His brother Angelo followed a similar path:

"To support his family, [...] he began playing music on the street again – just as he had done in his childhood. Angelo Kelly describes the time they lived in a trailer as intense but happy. Between 2011 and 2014, the family rambled around in Spain, Italy, France and Denmark [...]. His wife taught their children while Angelo went busking in the pedestrian zones. [...] It's all about the simple life, family bonds and the joy of making music."[2] Both Jimmy and his brother Angelo made use, although perhaps subconsciously, of the *reverse gap*. They turned their attention to what had worked well in the past, to that which made them happy.

These insights made it possible for them to plan and shape a future of fulfillment (*future gap*). They could happily forego the hype surrounding them in the nineties, and the lack of privacy they suffered back then was definitely not going to

[1]   Kelly, Jimmy, Streetkid: *Fluch und Segen, ein Kelly zu sein / The Curse and Blessing of Being a Kelly*, Heyne Verlag 2017, S. 11f.

[2]   stern.de, *Angelo Kellys Auswandererfamilie bringt Quotenrekord / Angelo Kelly's Expat Family Breaks Viewer Quotas*, 18.05.2016

happen again – they just wanted to make music, and nothing more. After a long break, the Kelly Family, down to six active members, once more gave concerts in larger venues. Angelo, however, had learned from the past, he would only play larger gigs. "…when we do so in a way that is healthy for all of us."[1]

Last year, during our junior employee program, we carried out a gap analysis with Jessica, a young leader. It was immediately clear to us that she was very eager to investigate the *reverse gap*. What really surprised us, though, were the results of her written analysis. After giving it plenty of thought, Jessica concluded she would give up her good and promising position in a pharmaceutical company and join her husband in the family business he had taken over from his father five years ago. Between finishing her studies and beginning her professional life, Jessica had worked in the business for three months and enjoyed it immensely. Even then, she had considered staying there and turning down the pharmaceutical company's offer. "But my husband and I thought it would be unreasonable to throw such a well-paid, promising career opportunity out the

_____

[1] Ibid.

window." Jessica wrote. "At least one of us should have a secure job, in case the family business didn't work out." Yet, there it stood, healthy and in need of her qualities. and to be honest, her current position did not bring the hoped-for fulfillment. This had nothing to do with the company, her salary and certainly not with her wonderful team – it just wasn't the right place for her, that certain something was missing. Jessica was so happy when the gap analysis gave her clarity and direction.

Closing the gap also means enjoying the moment. It means acknowledging the positive events in your life, no matter how small they may be. During our self-management coaching sessions and seminars, we recommend keeping a Book of Happiness. Every evening, before going to bed, write down five good things that made you happy that day. Pay extra attention to the tiny things; a smile from the supermarket cashier, your favorite song on the radio or a pat on the back from your boss.

Most participants have a tough time getting into the swing of it in the beginning but sticking with it eventually brings the desired results. Something nice happens to you and you immediately think, "This is one for my Book of Happiness!" You no longer need to comb through your entire day to find the positive events, you experience happiness the moment pleasant things happen. Your perception has changed focus, from a negative or neutral attitude, you have become positive. Consciously perceiving and taking pleasure in small events is simply a question of attentiveness. A Book of Happiness also has the advantage of sending you to sleep with positive thoughts, giving your subconscious something nice to work with.

In her feedback on one of our workshops, one participant – let's call her Felicia – wrote that it was her Book of Happiness that made her aware of how often she began her day with negative thoughts. This changed once she began consistently – every evening – to write down five good things that happened that day. "It wasn't long at all before I started waking up with a much more positive attitude," she wrote. Apparently, her subconscious quickly latched onto her focus on pleasant events. Felicia also discovered she could magnify the positive influence, what she called doubling the effect. Each morning, she recalled the positive events she had written down the evening before, which, she wrote to us, helped her greet the new day with even more positive energy and momentum.

Your Book of Happiness is an equally

supportive tool when things are not going so well. When all you can see are the wrong turns and poor judgments, a look in your Book of Happiness shows you another reality, turning your attention back to the basic pleasures in your life.

If you wish to redirect your focus, giving more attention to the present moment and positive events, get started right away with our Book of Happiness! You will find more information in this book's appendix.

There's no time like the present moment to begin writing down your moments of happiness! The following 100 pages invite you to take note of your happy moments for the next 100 days.

Day 1   Date: _____

1 _____

_____

_____

_____

2 _____

_____

_____

_____

3 _____

_____

_____

_____

4 _____

_____

_____

_____

5 _____

_____

_____

_____

Day 2   Date: _____

1 _____
_____
_____
_____

2 _____
_____
_____
_____

3 _____
_____
_____
_____

4 _____
_____
_____
_____

5 _____
_____
_____
_____

Day 3   Date: _____

1 _____
_____
_____
_____

2 _____
_____
_____
_____

3 _____
_____
_____
_____

4 _____
_____
_____
_____

5 _____
_____
_____
_____

Day 4   Date: _____

1 _____
_____
_____
_____

2 _____
_____
_____
_____

3 _____
_____
_____
_____

4 _____
_____
_____
_____

5 _____
_____
_____
_____

20

Day 5   Date: _____

1 _____
_____
_____
_____

2 _____
_____
_____
_____

3 _____
_____
_____
_____

4 _____
_____
_____
_____

5 _____
_____
_____
_____

Day 6   Date: _____

1 _____
_____
_____
_____

2 _____
_____
_____
_____

3 _____
_____
_____
_____

4 _____
_____
_____
_____

5 _____
_____
_____
_____

Day 7   Date: _____

1 _____
_____
_____
_____

2 _____
_____
_____
_____

3 _____
_____
_____
_____

4 _____
_____
_____
_____

5 _____
_____
_____
_____

Day 8   Date: _____

1 _____
_____
_____
_____

2 _____
_____
_____
_____

3 _____
_____
_____
_____

4 _____
_____
_____
_____

5 _____
_____
_____
_____

Day 9   Date: _____

1 _____
_____
_____
_____

2 _____
_____
_____
_____

3 _____
_____
_____
_____

4 _____
_____
_____
_____

5 _____
_____
_____
_____

Day 10   Date: _____

1 _____
_____
_____
_____

2 _____
_____
_____
_____

3 _____
_____
_____
_____

4 _____
_____
_____
_____

5 _____
_____
_____
_____

Day 11   Date: _____

1 _____
_____
_____
_____

2 _____
_____
_____
_____

3 _____
_____
_____
_____

4 _____
_____
_____
_____

5 _____
_____
_____
_____

Day 12   Date: _____

1 _____

_____

_____

_____

2 _____

_____

_____

_____

3 _____

_____

_____

_____

4 _____

_____

_____

_____

5 _____

_____

_____

_____

Day 13   Date: _____

1 _____
_____
_____
_____

2 _____
_____
_____
_____

3 _____
_____
_____
_____

4 _____
_____
_____
_____

5 _____
_____
_____
_____

Day 14   Date: _____

1 _____
_____
_____
_____

2 _____
_____
_____
_____

3 _____
_____
_____
_____

4 _____
_____
_____
_____

5 _____
_____
_____
_____

Day 15   Date: _____

1 _____
_____
_____
_____

2 _____
_____
_____
_____

3 _____
_____
_____
_____

4 _____
_____
_____
_____

5 _____
_____
_____
_____

Day 16   Date: _____

1 _____
_____
_____
_____

2 _____
_____
_____
_____

3 _____
_____
_____
_____

4 _____
_____
_____
_____

5 _____
_____
_____
_____

Day 17   Date: _____

1 _____
_____
_____
_____

2 _____
_____
_____
_____

3 _____
_____
_____
_____

4 _____
_____
_____
_____

5 _____
_____
_____
_____

Day 18   Date: _____

1 _____
_____
_____
_____

2 _____
_____
_____
_____

3 _____
_____
_____
_____

4 _____
_____
_____
_____

5 _____
_____
_____
_____

34

Day 19   Date: _____

1 _____
_____
_____
_____

2 _____
_____
_____
_____

3 _____
_____
_____
_____

4 _____
_____
_____
_____

5 _____
_____
_____
_____

Day 20   Date: _____

1 _____
_____
_____
_____

2 _____
_____
_____
_____

3 _____
_____
_____
_____

4 _____
_____
_____
_____

5 _____
_____
_____
_____

Day 21   Date: _____

1 _____
_____
_____
_____

2 _____
_____
_____
_____

3 _____
_____
_____
_____

4 _____
_____
_____
_____

5 _____
_____
_____
_____

Day 22   Date: _____

1 _____
_____
_____
_____

2 _____
_____
_____
_____

3 _____
_____
_____
_____

4 _____
_____
_____

5 _____
_____
_____

Day 23   Date: _____

1 _____

_____

_____

_____

2 _____

_____

_____

_____

3 _____

_____

_____

_____

4 _____

_____

_____

_____

5 _____

_____

_____

_____

Day 24   Date: _____

1 _____
_____
_____
_____

2 _____
_____
_____
_____

3 _____
_____
_____
_____

4 _____
_____
_____
_____

5 _____
_____
_____
_____

Day 25   Date: _____

1 _____
_____
_____
_____

2 _____
_____
_____
_____

3 _____
_____
_____
_____

4 _____
_____
_____
_____

5 _____
_____
_____
_____

Day 26   Date: _____

1 _____
_____
_____
_____

2 _____
_____
_____
_____

3 _____
_____
_____
_____

4 _____
_____
_____
_____

5 _____
_____
_____
_____

Day 27   Date: _____

1 _____
_____
_____
_____

2 _____
_____
_____
_____

3 _____
_____
_____
_____

4 _____
_____
_____
_____

5 _____
_____
_____
_____

Day 28   Date: _____

1 _____
_____
_____
_____

2 _____
_____
_____
_____

3 _____
_____
_____
_____

4 _____
_____
_____
_____

5 _____
_____
_____
_____

Day 29   Date: _____

1 _____
_____
_____
_____

2 _____
_____
_____
_____

3 _____
_____
_____
_____

4 _____
_____
_____
_____

5 _____
_____
_____
_____

Day 30   Date: _____

1 _____
_____
_____
_____

2 _____
_____
_____
_____

3 _____
_____
_____
_____

4 _____
_____
_____
_____

5 _____
_____
_____
_____

Day 31   Date: _____

1 _____
_____
_____
_____

2 _____
_____
_____
_____

3 _____
_____
_____
_____

4 _____
_____
_____
_____

5 _____
_____
_____
_____

Day 32   Date: _____

1 _____
_____
_____
_____

2 _____
_____
_____
_____

3 _____
_____
_____
_____

4 _____
_____
_____
_____

5 _____
_____
_____
_____

Day 33   Date: _____

1 _____
_____
_____
_____

2 _____
_____
_____
_____

3 _____
_____
_____
_____

4 _____
_____
_____
_____

5 _____
_____
_____
_____

Day 34   Date: _____

1 _____
_____
_____
_____

2 _____
_____
_____
_____

3 _____
_____
_____
_____

4 _____
_____
_____
_____

5 _____
_____
_____
_____

Day 35   Date: _____

1 _____
_____
_____
_____

2 _____
_____
_____
_____

3 _____
_____
_____
_____

4 _____
_____
_____
_____

5 _____
_____
_____
_____

Day 36   Date: _____

1 _____
_____
_____
_____

2 _____
_____
_____
_____

3 _____
_____
_____
_____

4 _____
_____
_____
_____

5 _____
_____
_____
_____

Day 37   Date: _____

1 _____
_____
_____
_____

2 _____
_____
_____
_____

3 _____
_____
_____
_____

4 _____
_____
_____
_____

5 _____
_____
_____
_____

Day 38   Date: _____

1 _____
_____
_____
_____

2 _____
_____
_____
_____

3 _____
_____
_____
_____

4 _____
_____
_____
_____

5 _____
_____
_____
_____

Day 39   Date: _____

1 _____
_____
_____
_____

2 _____
_____
_____
_____

3 _____
_____
_____
_____

4 _____
_____
_____
_____

5 _____
_____
_____
_____

Day 40   Date: _____

1 _____
_____
_____
_____

2 _____
_____
_____
_____

3 _____
_____
_____
_____

4 _____
_____
_____
_____

5 _____
_____
_____
_____

Day 41   Date: _____

1 _____
_____
_____
_____

2 _____
_____
_____
_____

3 _____
_____
_____
_____

4 _____
_____
_____
_____

5 _____
_____
_____
_____

Day 42   Date: _____

1 _____
_____
_____
_____

2 _____
_____
_____
_____

3 _____
_____
_____
_____

4 _____
_____
_____
_____

5 _____
_____
_____
_____

Day 43   Date: _____

1 _____
_____
_____
_____

2 _____
_____
_____
_____

3 _____
_____
_____
_____

4 _____
_____
_____
_____

5 _____
_____
_____
_____

Day 44   Date: _____

1 _____
_____
_____
_____

2 _____
_____
_____
_____

3 _____
_____
_____
_____

4 _____
_____
_____
_____

5 _____
_____
_____
_____

Day 45   Date: _____

1 _____
_____
_____
_____

2 _____
_____
_____
_____

3 _____
_____
_____
_____

4 _____
_____
_____
_____

5 _____
_____
_____
_____

Day 46   Date: _____

1 _____
_____
_____
_____

2 _____
_____
_____
_____

3 _____
_____
_____
_____

4 _____
_____
_____
_____

5 _____
_____
_____
_____

Day 47   Date: _____

1 _____
_____
_____
_____

2 _____
_____
_____
_____

3 _____
_____
_____
_____

4 _____
_____
_____
_____

5 _____
_____
_____
_____

Day 48   Date: _____

1 _____
_____
_____
_____

2 _____
_____
_____
_____

3 _____
_____
_____
_____

4 _____
_____
_____
_____

5 _____
_____
_____
_____

Day 49   Date: _____

1 _____
_____
_____
_____

2 _____
_____
_____
_____

3 _____
_____
_____
_____

4 _____
_____
_____
_____

5 _____
_____
_____
_____

Day 50   Date: _____

1 _____
_____
_____
_____

2 _____
_____
_____
_____

3 _____
_____
_____
_____

4 _____
_____
_____
_____

5 _____
_____
_____
_____

Day 51   Date: _____

1 _____
_____
_____
_____

2 _____
_____
_____
_____

3 _____
_____
_____
_____

4 _____
_____
_____
_____

5 _____
_____
_____
_____

Day 52   Date: _____

1 _____
_____
_____
_____

2 _____
_____
_____
_____

3 _____
_____
_____
_____

4 _____
_____
_____
_____

5 _____
_____
_____
_____

Day 53   Date: _____

1 _____

_____

_____

_____

2 _____

_____

_____

_____

3 _____

_____

_____

_____

4 _____

_____

_____

_____

5 _____

_____

_____

_____

Day 54   Date: _____

1 _____
_____
_____
_____

2 _____
_____
_____
_____

3 _____
_____
_____
_____

4 _____
_____
_____
_____

5 _____
_____
_____
_____

Day 55   Date: _____

1 _____

_____

_____

_____

2 _____

_____

_____

_____

3 _____

_____

_____

_____

4 _____

_____

_____

_____

5 _____

_____

_____

_____

Day 56   Date: _____

1 _____
_____
_____
_____

2 _____
_____
_____
_____

3 _____
_____
_____
_____

4 _____
_____
_____
_____

5 _____
_____
_____
_____

Day 57   Date: _____

1 _____
_____
_____
_____

2 _____
_____
_____
_____

3 _____
_____
_____
_____

4 _____
_____
_____
_____

5 _____
_____
_____
_____

Day 58   Date: _____

1 _____
_____
_____
_____

2 _____
_____
_____
_____

3 _____
_____
_____
_____

4 _____
_____
_____
_____

5 _____
_____
_____
_____

Day 59   Date: _____

1 _____
_____
_____
_____

2 _____
_____
_____
_____

3 _____
_____
_____
_____

4 _____
_____
_____
_____

5 _____
_____
_____
_____

Day 60   Date: _____

1 _____
_____
_____
_____

2 _____
_____
_____
_____

3 _____
_____
_____
_____

4 _____
_____
_____
_____

5 _____
_____
_____
_____

Day 61   Date: _____

1 _____
  _____
  _____
  _____

2 _____
  _____
  _____
  _____

3 _____
  _____
  _____
  _____

4 _____
  _____
  _____
  _____

5 _____
  _____
  _____
  _____

Day 62   Date: _____

1 _____
_____
_____
_____

2 _____
_____
_____
_____

3 _____
_____
_____
_____

4 _____
_____
_____
_____

5 _____
_____
_____
_____

Day 63   Date: _____

1 _____
  _____
  _____
  _____

2 _____
  _____
  _____
  _____

3 _____
  _____
  _____
  _____

4 _____
  _____
  _____
  _____

5 _____
  _____
  _____
  _____

Day 64   Date: _____

1 _____
_____
_____
_____

2 _____
_____
_____
_____

3 _____
_____
_____
_____

4 _____
_____
_____
_____

5 _____
_____
_____
_____

Day 65   Date: _____

1 _____

_____

_____

_____

2 _____

_____

_____

_____

3 _____

_____

_____

_____

4 _____

_____

_____

_____

5 _____

_____

_____

_____

Day 66   Date: _____

1 _____
_____
_____
_____

2 _____
_____
_____
_____

3 _____
_____
_____
_____

4 _____
_____
_____
_____

5 _____
_____
_____
_____

Day 67   Date: _____

1 _____
_____
_____
_____

2 _____
_____
_____
_____

3 _____
_____
_____
_____

4 _____
_____
_____
_____

5 _____
_____
_____
_____

Day 68   Date: _____

1 _____
_____
_____
_____

2 _____
_____
_____
_____

3 _____
_____
_____
_____

4 _____
_____
_____
_____

5 _____
_____
_____
_____

Day 69   Date: _____

1 _____
_____
_____
_____

2 _____
_____
_____
_____

3 _____
_____
_____
_____

4 _____
_____
_____
_____

5 _____
_____
_____
_____

Day 70   Date: _____

1 _____
_____
_____
_____

2 _____
_____
_____
_____

3 _____
_____
_____
_____

4 _____
_____
_____
_____

5 _____
_____
_____
_____

Day 71   Date: _____

1 _____

_____

_____

_____

2 _____

_____

_____

_____

3 _____

_____

_____

_____

4 _____

_____

_____

_____

5 _____

_____

_____

_____

Day 72   Date: _____

1 _____
_____
_____
_____

2 _____
_____
_____
_____

3 _____
_____
_____
_____

4 _____
_____
_____
_____

5 _____
_____
_____
_____

Day 73   Date: _____

1 _____
_____
_____
_____

2 _____
_____
_____
_____

3 _____
_____
_____
_____

4 _____
_____
_____
_____

5 _____
_____
_____
_____

Day 74   Date: _____

1 _____
_____
_____
_____

2 _____
_____
_____
_____

3 _____
_____
_____
_____

4 _____
_____
_____
_____

5 _____
_____
_____
_____

Day 75   Date: _____

1 _____
_____
_____
_____

2 _____
_____
_____
_____

3 _____
_____
_____
_____

4 _____
_____
_____
_____

5 _____
_____
_____
_____

Day 76   Date: _____

1 _____
_____
_____
_____

2 _____
_____
_____
_____

3 _____
_____
_____
_____

4 _____
_____
_____
_____

5 _____
_____
_____
_____

Day 77   Date: _____

1 _____
_____
_____
_____

2 _____
_____
_____
_____

3 _____
_____
_____
_____

4 _____
_____
_____
_____

5 _____
_____
_____
_____

Day 78   Date: _____

1 _____
_____
_____
_____

2 _____
_____
_____
_____

3 _____
_____
_____
_____

4 _____
_____
_____
_____

5 _____
_____
_____
_____

Day 79   Date: _____

1 _____
_____
_____
_____

2 _____
_____
_____
_____

3 _____
_____
_____
_____

4 _____
_____
_____
_____

5 _____
_____
_____
_____

Day 80   Date: _____

1 _____
_____
_____
_____

2 _____
_____
_____
_____

3 _____
_____
_____
_____

4 _____
_____
_____
_____

5 _____
_____
_____
_____

Day 81   Date: _____

1 _____
_____
_____
_____

2 _____
_____
_____
_____

3 _____
_____
_____
_____

4 _____
_____
_____
_____

5 _____
_____
_____
_____

Day 82   Date: _____

1 _____
_____
_____
_____

2 _____
_____
_____
_____

3 _____
_____
_____
_____

4 _____
_____
_____
_____

5 _____
_____
_____
_____

Day 83   Date: _____

1 _____
_____
_____
_____

2 _____
_____
_____
_____

3 _____
_____
_____
_____

4 _____
_____
_____
_____

5 _____
_____
_____
_____

Day 84   Date: _____

1 _____
_____
_____
_____

2 _____
_____
_____
_____

3 _____
_____
_____
_____

4 _____
_____
_____
_____

5 _____
_____
_____
_____

Day 85   Date: _____

1 _____
_____
_____
_____

2 _____
_____
_____
_____

3 _____
_____
_____
_____

4 _____
_____
_____
_____

5 _____
_____
_____
_____

Day 86   Date: _____

1 _____
_____
_____
_____

2 _____
_____
_____
_____

3 _____
_____
_____
_____

4 _____
_____
_____
_____

5 _____
_____
_____
_____

Day 87

Date: _____

1 _____
_____
_____
_____

2 _____
_____
_____
_____

3 _____
_____
_____
_____

4 _____
_____
_____
_____

5 _____
_____
_____
_____

Day 88   Date: _____

1 _____
_____
_____
_____

2 _____
_____
_____
_____

3 _____
_____
_____
_____

4 _____
_____
_____
_____

5 _____
_____
_____
_____

Day 89   Date: _____

1 _____
_____
_____
_____

2 _____
_____
_____
_____

3 _____
_____
_____
_____

4 _____
_____
_____
_____

5 _____
_____
_____
_____

Day 90   Date: _____

1 _____
_____
_____
_____

2 _____
_____
_____
_____

3 _____
_____
_____
_____

4 _____
_____
_____
_____

5 _____
_____
_____
_____

Day 91   Date: _____

1 _____

_____

_____

_____

2 _____

_____

_____

_____

3 _____

_____

_____

_____

4 _____

_____

_____

_____

5 _____

_____

_____

_____

Day 92   Date: _____

1 _____
_____
_____
_____

2 _____
_____
_____
_____

3 _____
_____
_____
_____

4 _____
_____
_____
_____

5 _____
_____
_____
_____

Day 93   Date: _____

1 _____
_____
_____
_____

2 _____
_____
_____
_____

3 _____
_____
_____
_____

4 _____
_____
_____
_____

5 _____
_____
_____
_____

Day 94   Date: _____

1 _____
_____
_____
_____

2 _____
_____
_____
_____

3 _____
_____
_____
_____

4 _____
_____
_____
_____

5 _____
_____
_____
_____

Day 95   Date: _____

1 _____
_____
_____
_____

2 _____
_____
_____
_____

3 _____
_____
_____
_____

4 _____
_____
_____
_____

5 _____
_____
_____
_____

Day 96   Date: _____

1 _____
_____
_____
_____

2 _____
_____
_____
_____

3 _____
_____
_____
_____

4 _____
_____
_____
_____

5 _____
_____
_____
_____

Day 97   Date: _____

1 _____
_____
_____
_____

2 _____
_____
_____
_____

3 _____
_____
_____
_____

4 _____
_____
_____
_____

5 _____
_____
_____
_____

Day 98   Date: _____

1 _____
_____
_____
_____

2 _____
_____
_____
_____

3 _____
_____
_____
_____

4 _____
_____
_____
_____

5 _____
_____
_____
_____

Day 99   Date: _____

1 _____
_____
_____
_____

2 _____
_____
_____
_____

3 _____
_____
_____
_____

4 _____
_____
_____
_____

5 _____
_____
_____
_____

Day 100   Date: _____

1 _____
_____
_____
_____

2 _____
_____
_____
_____

3 _____
_____
_____
_____

4 _____
_____
_____
_____

5 _____
_____
_____
_____

The Authors

Marcello, Gianni und Jan Liscia (left to right)

Since its inception in 2000, taking shape in Paderborn, Germany, the name Liscia Consulting has gained ground on both national and international terrain with their excellent work in leader development. A most competent partner for strategy, conception and getting things done.

Business leaders Gianni, Marcello and Jan Liscia are not your everyday seminar conductors. Nor are they generic trainers or coaches. Gianni, Marcello and Jan Liscia are consultants who train and coach leaders. They are strategic partners, guiding and mediating transitional processes.

www.Liscia-Consulting.com

Keynote presentation for your event

On the pulse of change with inspiring keynote lectures! A keynote presentation can be designed to run 30 minutes or up to 3 hours – according to your event's agenda!

Together, we determine the focus of your D.R.E.A.M. of LEADERS® keynote lecture, i.e. Employee Engagement in Global Leadership, Transitional Process Leadership or Digital Leadership. Our multifarious and unusual approach infuses your business with new impulses, creating an atmosphere of awakening and a desire for change.

A rational/emotional composition coupled with the blunt, stark reality of our times invokes profound reflection. To easier digest discomfiting truth, we served it with a healthy portion of humor.

www.Liscia-Consulting.com

Herman, illustrator

Herman, illustrator

Herman is, and has been for some time, one of the most high-profile, successful pop art painters of our time. His edgy, idiosyncratic graphics and pictures are downright bodacious. Once a trained screen printer, his unleashed creativity has astonished viewers at over 200 national and international exhibits. Herman has been an independent artist since 1991. Over the past years, the name Herman can also be found under cartoons drawn for a variety of German publishing houses. His flying heart comic strip in Bravo, a German youth magazine, was published several consecutive years, becoming a household name. The same can be said of the 18 Herman collector's glasses commissioned by Ritzenhoff. In 2007, bids were made for 49 Herman paintings at a charity auction benefiting the Peter Maffay Foundation.

www.Kuenstler-Herman.com

Want more? Here's an overview of all books by Gianni, Jan & Marcello Liscia:

Gianni, Jan & Marcello Liscia

D.R.E.A.M.
of
LEADERS

Leadership is not an Illusion

Illustrations:
Herman Reichold

ISBN: 978-3-744-88271-2 – 19,90 € (D), E-Book: 14,99 € (D)

All of our titles are available as ebooks (except The Book of Happiness) and can be enjoyed in the German language, too!

Gianni, Jan & Marcello Liscia

WORKBOOK
DEDICATION

Dedication to the work at hand, with heart and soul.
24 hours a day

Illustrations:
Herman Reichold

ISBN: 978-3-7528-5787-0
8,90 € (D), E-Book: 4,99 € (D)

Gianni, Jan & Marcello Liscia

WORKBOOK
RESPONSIBILITY

Showing responsibility for decisions made, for employees
and for oneself

Illustrations:
Herman Reichold

ISBN: 978-3-7528-5825-9
8,90 € (D), E-Book: 4,99 € (D)

Gianni, Jan & Marcello Liscia

WORKBOOK
EDUCATION

Personal and employee education

Illustrations:
Herman Reichold

ISBN: 978-3-7528-5826-6
8,90 € (D), E-Book: 4,99 € (D)

Gianni, Jan & Marcello Liscia

WORKBOOK
ATTITUDE

A question of personal attitude and values which are
lived and experienced

Illustrations:
Herman Reichold

ISBN: 978-3-7528-5827-3
8,90 € (D), E-Book: 4,99 € (D)

Gianni, Jan & Marcello Liscia

WORKBOOK
MOTIVATION

Being ready to perform is the basis for all action

Illustrations:
Herman Reichold

ISBN: 978-3-7528-5828-0
8,90 € (D), E-Book: 4,99 € (D)